HOW TO DRAW
SHIPS

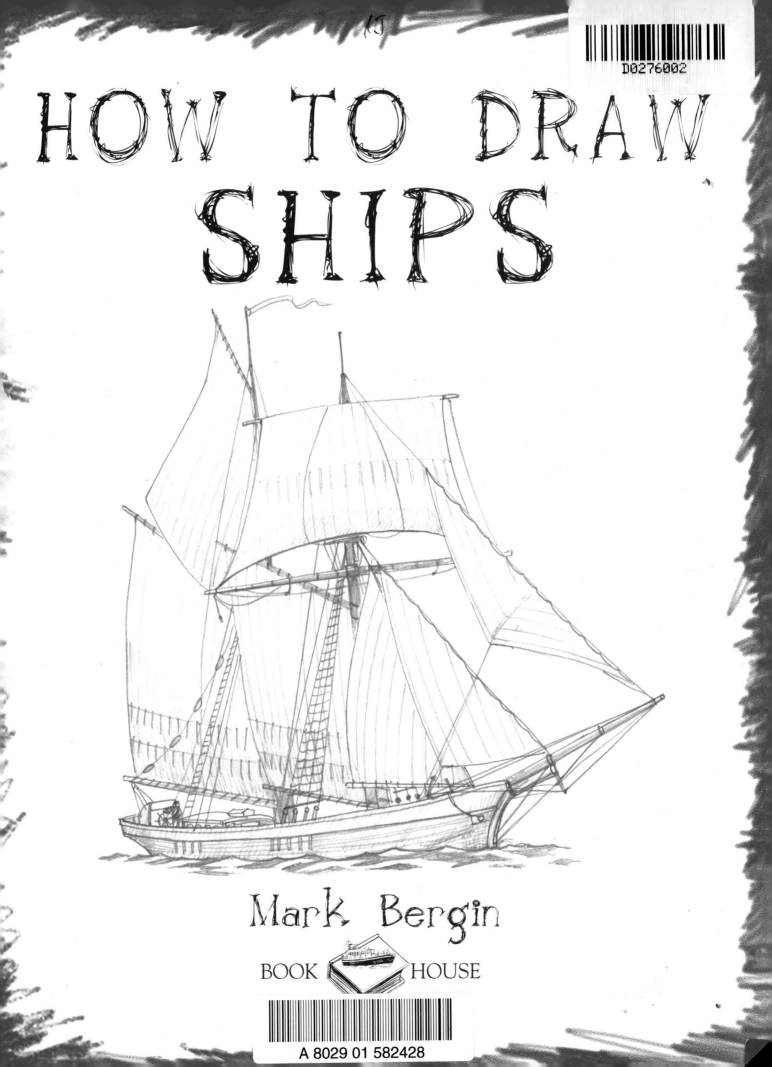

Mark Bergin

BOOK HOUSE

SALARIYA

Published in Great Britain in 2008 by
Book House, an imprint of
The Salariya Book Company Ltd
25 Marlborough Place, Brighton BN1 1UB

1 3 5 7 9 8 6 4 2

Please visit our website at **www.salariya.com**
for **free** electronic versions of:
You Wouldn't Want to Be an Egyptian Mummy!
You Wouldn't Want to Be a Roman Gladiator!
Avoid Joining Shackleton's Polar Expedition!
Avoid Sailing on a 19th-Century Whaling Ship!

Author: Mark Bergin was born in Hastings in 1961.
He studied at Eastbourne College of Art and has
specialised in historical reconstructions as well as
aviation and maritime subjects since 1983. He lives
in Bexhill-on-Sea with his wife and three children.

Editor: Rob Walker

PB ISBN: 978-1-906370-34-3

A CIP catalogue record for this
book is available from the
British Library.

Printed and bound in China.
Printed on paper from
sustainable sources.

**WARNING: Fixatives should be
used only under adult supervision.**

PAPER FROM
**SUSTAINABLE
FORESTS**

Contents

Making a start

Learning to draw is about looking and seeing. Keep practising, and get to know your subject. Use a sketchbook to make quick sketches. Start by doodling, and experiment with shapes and patterns. There are many ways to draw; this book shows some of them. Visit art galleries, look at artists' drawings, see how friends draw, but above all, find your own way.

Pencil

Large felt-tip pen

4

Ballpoint pen

Remember that practice makes
perfect. If it looks wrong, start again.
Keep working at it — the more you
draw, the more you will learn.

Fine liner pen

Felt-tip pen

5

Perspective

If you look at any object from different viewpoints, you will see that the part that is closest to you looks larger, and the part furthest away from you looks smaller. Drawing in perspective is a way of creating a feeling of depth — of showing three dimensions on a flat surface.

It may help you with perspective if you imagine your object fitted into a rectangular block like this.

V.P.

The vanishing point (V.P.) is the place in a perspective drawing where parallel lines appear to meet. The position of the vanishing point depends on the viewer's eye level. Sometimes a low viewpoint can give your drawing added drama.

Two-point perspective uses two vanishing points: one for lines running along the length of the object, and one on the opposite side for lines running across the width of the object.

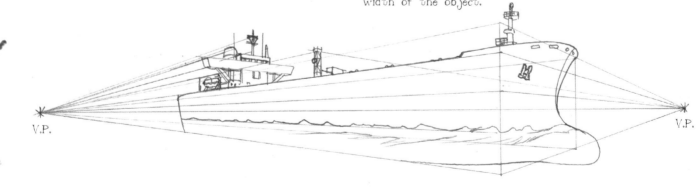

V.P.   V.P.

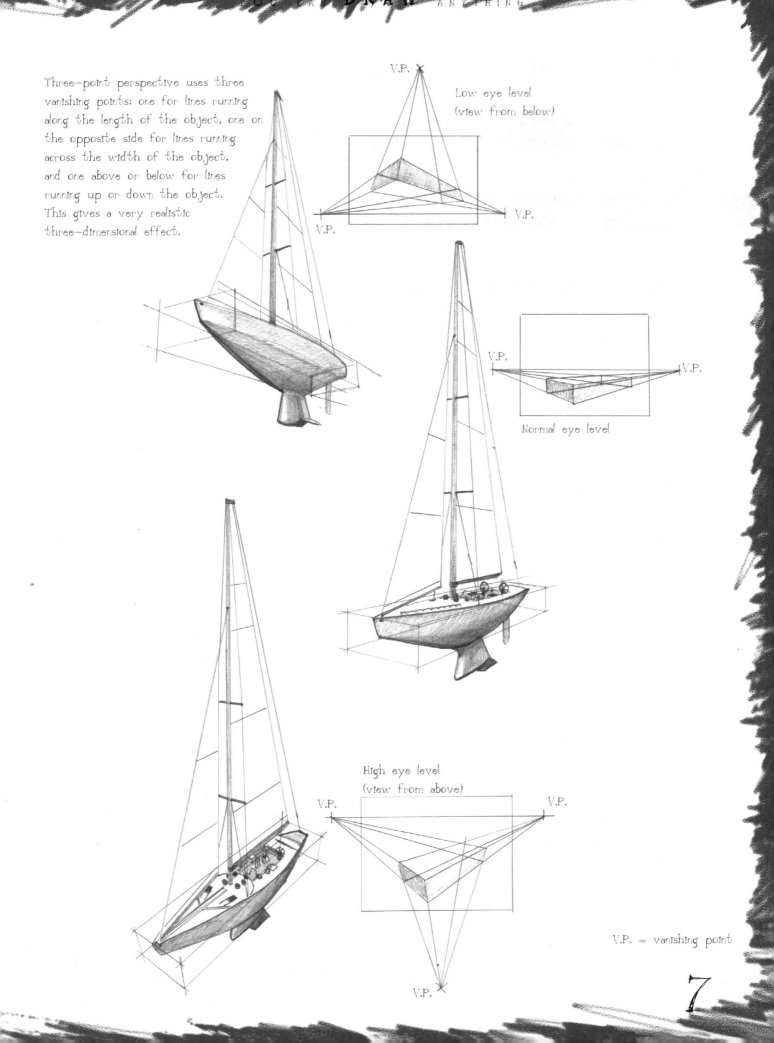

Three—point perspective uses three vanishing points: one for lines running along the length of the object, one on the opposite side for lines running across the width of the object, and one above or below for lines running up or down the object. This gives a very realistic three—dimensional effect.

Low eye level
(view from below)

V.P.

V.P.

V.P.

Normal eye level

V.P.

V.P.

High eye level
(view from above)

V.P.

V.P.

V.P. = vanishing point

V.P.

7

Photographs

Drawing from photographs can help you practise your drawing skills. It is important that you consider the position of your drawing on the paper; this is called composition.

Make a tracing of the photograph.

Grids

Using a grid to help you enlarge a drawing is called squaring up.

Lightly draw a grid over your traced image.

8

Light source

Decide which direction the light is coming from in your drawing. Add shadows on the parts of the ship that face away from the light.

Lightly draw a grid on your drawing paper, using larger squares than before but keeping the same proportions. You can now copy the shapes in each square of your tracing onto your drawing paper.

Add more tone and detail to finish the drawing.

Add a background to give atmosphere to your drawing.

9

Drawing sails

Sails are large pieces of fabric used to catch the wind to propel a boat or ship. The shape of a sail changes depending on how the wind catches it.

Here you can see how the shape of a sail changes depending on the direction of the wind.

Wind direction

Wind direction

Wind direction

There are many different
types of sailing craft.
There is huge variation in
the shape, the number of
sails and the formation
they take.

Bermuda rig

Sloop

Yawl or ketch

Spritsail barge

Schooner

Brigantine

Topsail schooner

Brig

Square-rigged ship

Large racing yachts

11

Sketching

You can't always rely on your memory, so you have to look around and find real-life things you want to draw. Using a sketchbook is one of the best ways to build up drawing skills. Learn to observe objects: see how they move, how they are made and how they work. What you draw should be what you have seen. Since the 15th century, artists have used sketchbooks to record their ideas.

Sketching models

Try drawing model ships and boats. You can look closely and start to understand your subject.

A harbour is a good place to start. There are many different types of boats that you can draw in an interesting setting.

Sketching

A quick sketch can often capture as much information as a careful drawing that has taken many hours.

Speedboat

Speedboats are designed to move quickly through the water. They are propelled by powerful motors at the stern.

First draw a three—dimensional rectangular box. Then draw a line through the centre.

Using the centre line as a starting point, draw long curved lines to show the shape of the boat.

The stern (rear) of the boat is drawn in with straight lines.

Draw straight lines on the bottom of the rectangular box to mark the bottom of the boat.

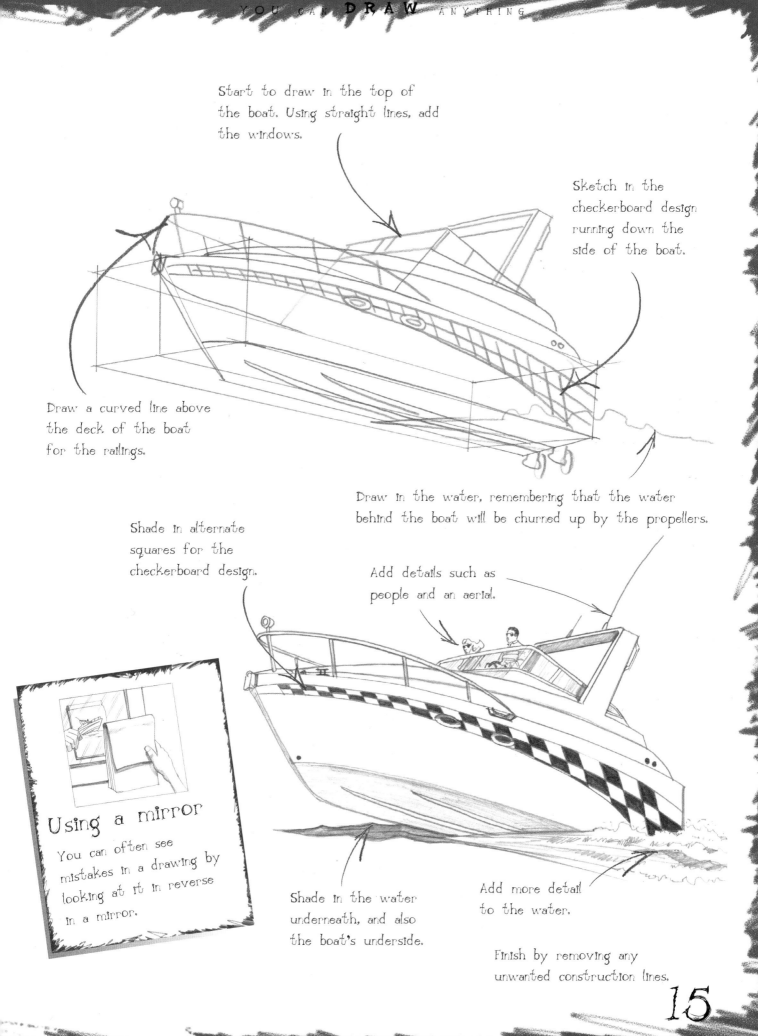

Start to draw in the top of the boat. Using straight lines, add the windows.

Sketch in the checkerboard design running down the side of the boat.

Draw a curved line above the deck of the boat for the railings.

Draw in the water, remembering that the water behind the boat will be churned up by the propellers.

Shade in alternate squares for the checkerboard design.

Add details such as people and an aerial.

Using a mirror

You can often see mistakes in a drawing by looking at it in reverse in a mirror.

Shade in the water underneath, and also the boat's underside.

Add more detail to the water.

Finish by removing any unwanted construction lines.

Racing yacht

Yacht races are held all around the world. The yachts used are specially designed to take full advantage of the wind and move very fast through the water.

Mast

Draw two long lines for the mast.

Start by drawing a narrow rectangle for the hull.

Draw in a straight line for the water.

Add a line to form a small triangle to make the stern of the boat.

Draw a straight line down from the mast to the bow (front) of the boat.

Add a straight line coming down from the top of the mast to the stern of the boat.

Add curves to the bow of the boat.

Add the keel.

Add a small rudder.

Draw in the head sail of the boat using curv
lines. The wind is blowing from behind the bo
filling the sail so it bulges forwards.

Add the mainsail of the boat.

Head sail

Add in the wavy waterline.

Mainsail

Draw in the stripes
on the hull.

Keel

Composition
Framing your drawing with a
square or rectangle can make
it look completely different.

Draw details on
the head sail.

Add details to
the mainsail.

GBR
41R

Shade in areas of the
head sail.

Put people on the boat.

Shade the
water to look
like waves.

Finish the details on
the boat.

Remove any unwanted
construction lines.

17

rowing boat

This traditional rowing boat is a small craft made out of wood. It needs oars to propel it through the water.

First draw a three-dimensional box with a centre line through its mid-section.

Inside this box, draw curved lines to form the shape of the boat. The stern should be the same height as the box, but the bow rises above it.

The keel on a rowing boat runs its entire length. Add it in with curved lines.

Draw a long curved line for the bottom of the boat.

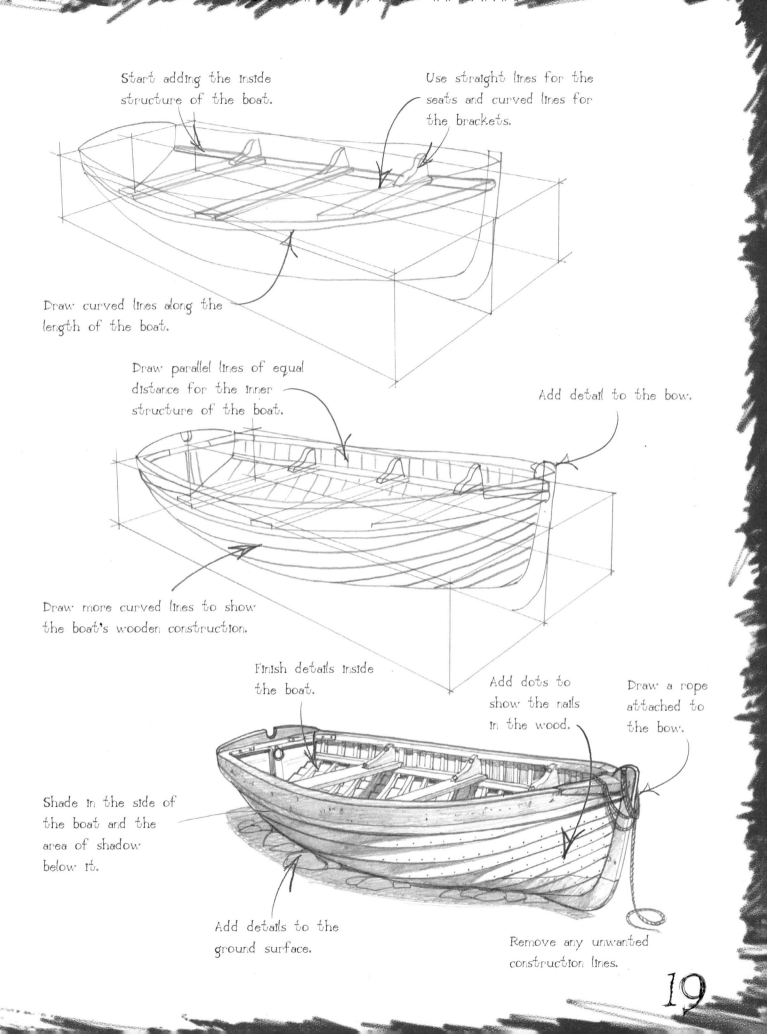

Start adding the inside structure of the boat.

Use straight lines for the seats and curved lines for the brackets.

Draw curved lines along the length of the boat.

Draw parallel lines of equal distance for the inner structure of the boat.

Add detail to the bow.

Draw more curved lines to show the boat's wooden construction.

Finish details inside the boat.

Add dots to show the nails in the wood.

Draw a rope attached to the bow.

Shade in the side of the boat and the area of shadow below it.

Add details to the ground surface.

Remove any unwanted construction lines.

19

Topsail schooner

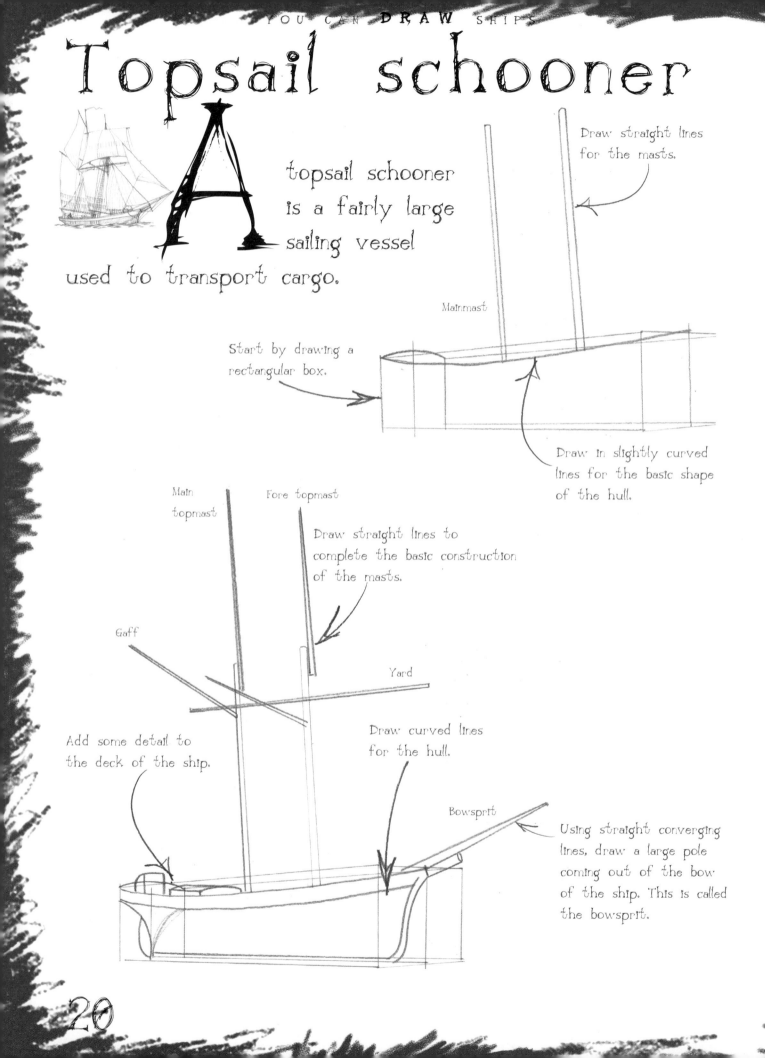

A topsail schooner is a fairly large sailing vessel used to transport cargo.

Draw straight lines for the masts.

Mainmast

Start by drawing a rectangular box.

Draw in slightly curved lines for the basic shape of the hull.

Main topmast

Fore topmast

Draw straight lines to complete the basic construction of the masts.

Gaff

Yard

Add some detail to the deck of the ship.

Draw curved lines for the hull.

Bowsprit

Using straight converging lines, draw a large pole coming out of the bow of the ship. This is called the bowsprit.

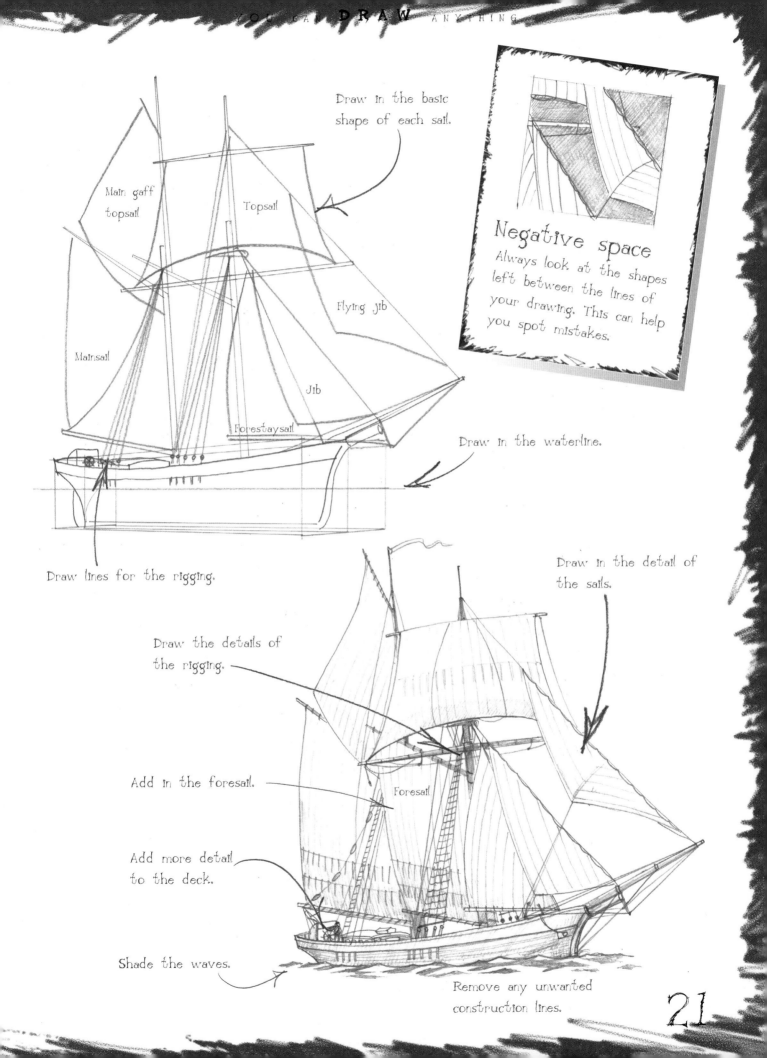

Main gaff
topsail

Topsail

Draw in the basic
shape of each sail.

Flying jib

Mainsail

Jib

Forestaysail

Negative space
Always look at the shapes
left between the lines of
your drawing. This can help
you spot mistakes.

Draw in the waterline.

Draw lines for the rigging.

Draw the details of
the rigging.

Draw in the detail of
the sails.

Add in the foresail.

Foresail

Add more detail
to the deck.

Shade the waves.

Remove any unwanted
construction lines.

21

Ocean tanker

An ocean tanker is a massive ship used to transport huge amounts of fuel.

Ships and water

To make your drawing look authentic: the ship should always be sitting in the water, not on top of it.

Start your drawing with a large rectangular box with a centre line through the mid-section.

Draw a curved lip to indicate the top of the bow.

Using the lines of your original rectangular box as a guide, draw box shapes on the ship's deck where the superstructure will be.

Draw curved lines to mark the shape of the ship's bow.

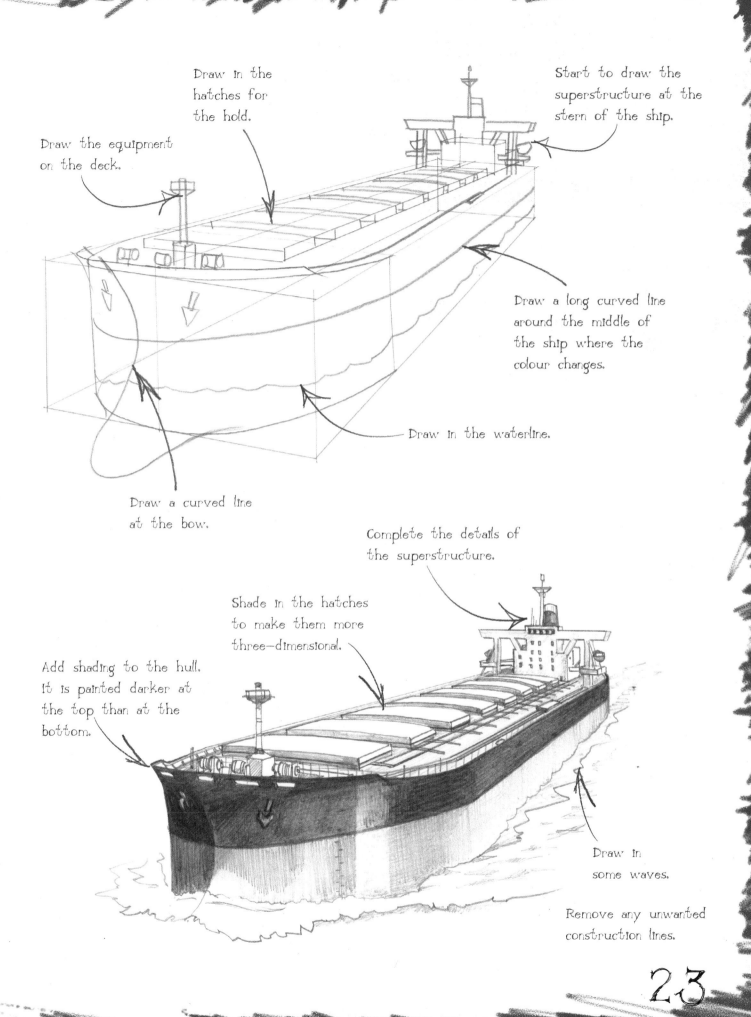

Draw in the
hatches for
the hold.

Draw the equipment
on the deck.

Start to draw the
superstructure at the
stern of the ship.

Draw a long curved line
around the middle of
the ship where the
colour changes.

Draw in the waterline.

Draw a curved line
at the bow.

Complete the details of
the superstructure.

Shade in the hatches
to make them more
three-dimensional.

Add shading to the hull.
It is painted darker at
the top than at the
bottom.

Draw in
some waves.

Remove any unwanted
construction lines.

23

Fishing boat

This small fishing boat is a working vessel that travels out to sea to try to catch a good haul of fish.

Start your drawing with a three-dimensional rectangular box with a centre line through the mid-section.

Begin the main hull of the boat by drawing curved lines. The stern is the same height as the box, but the bow rises above it.

Add a curved line for the stern of the boat.

The keel for this boat curves down the bow but straightens along the bottom of the hull.

Add a small house-like structure at the bow.

Add the main bridge structure to the deck.

Add more curved lines to the side of the boat.

Draw straight lines for the ropes of the fishing equipment.

Use straight lines to draw in the arms of the fishing equipment.

Draw in the winch machinery.

Add detail to the bridge.

Darken the underside of the lines on the side of the boat to give a realistic shadow effect.

Add in the water surface.

Remove any unwanted construction lines.

25

Ocean liner

This luxury ocean liner is a large sea-going vessel designed to transport many people in great comfort.

Draw a centre line through the mid-section.

Start by drawing a long rectangular box in perspective.

Add another box in perspective for the main part of the superstructure.

Draw two lines curving towards the centre line for the bow of the ship.

Add curved lines for the hull.

Draw the curvy line that makes up the bow of the ship.

Add the funnels.

Add detail to the front of the main superstructure.

Draw in the waterline.

Add guidelines along the upper decks to help you position the windows.

Sketch in a line for the window of the bridge.

Add in small shapes for the lifeboats.

Using the straight lines as a guide, finish the detail of the windows.

Complete the details of the superstructure.

Add tone to the drawing to give it more impact.

Add in small dots for the portholes.

Add small areas of shading to represent the waves.

Remove any unwanted construction lines.

27

Lifeboat

Lifeboats play a crucial
role along coastal areas.
These boats need to be
fast, steady and durable to carry out
rescues in difficult conditions.

First draw a
perspective box
with a centre line
down the middle.

Add another three—
dimensional box for
the cabin on the deck.

Use straight lines
for the front
section of the cabin.

Add a curved line
to create the bow.

Draw a straight
line for the front
of the bow.

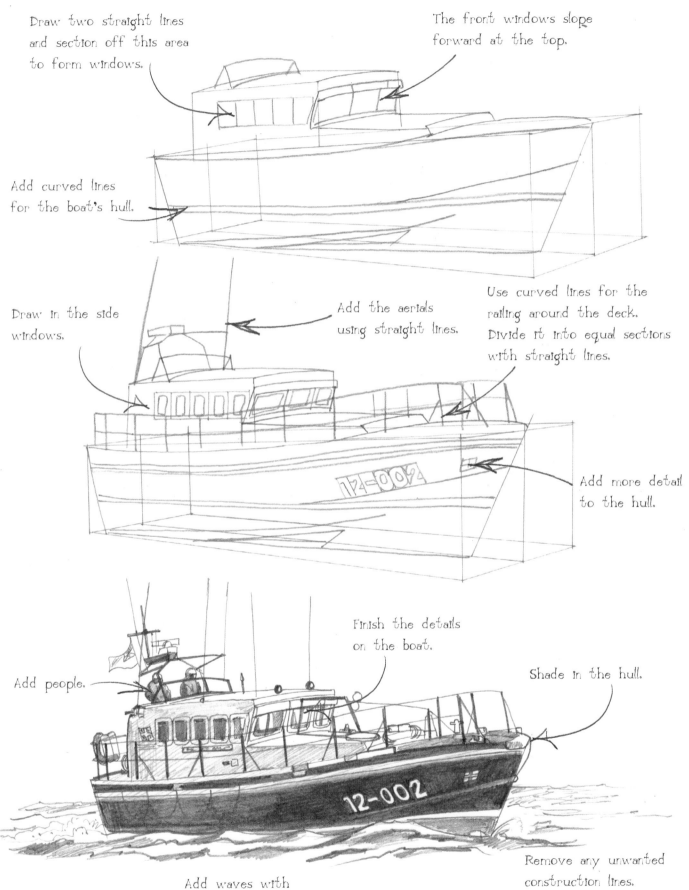

Draw two straight lines
and section off this area
to form windows.

The front windows slope
forward at the top.

Add curved lines
for the boat's hull.

Draw in the side
windows.

Add the aerials
using straight lines.

Use curved lines for the
railing around the deck.
Divide it into equal sections
with straight lines.

Add more detail
to the hull.

Finish the details
on the boat.

Shade in the hull.

Add people.

12-002

Add waves with
sketchy lines and shading.

Remove any unwanted
construction lines.

29

Harbour scene

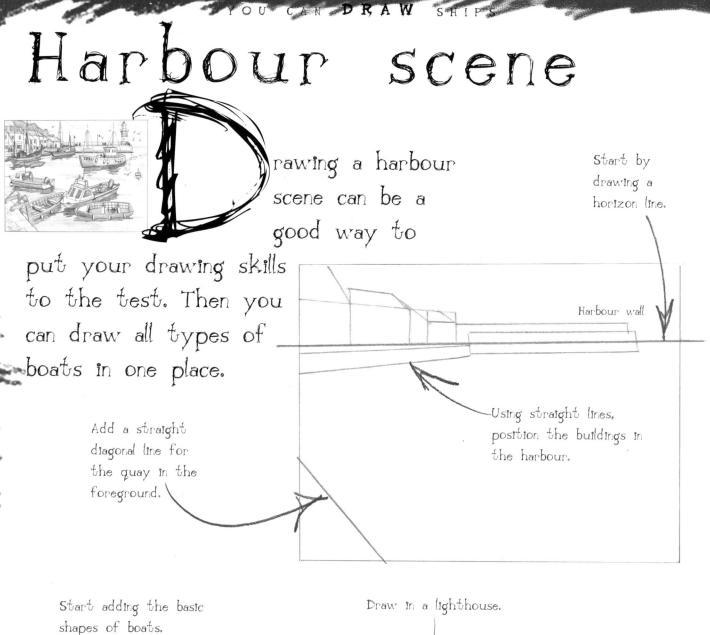

Drawing a harbour scene can be a good way to put your drawing skills to the test. Then you can draw all types of boats in one place.

Start by drawing a horizon line.

Harbour wall

Using straight lines, position the buildings in the harbour.

Add a straight diagonal line for the quay in the foreground.

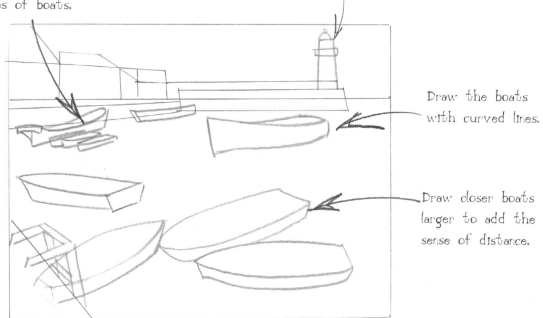

Start adding the basic shapes of boats.

Draw in a lighthouse.

Draw the boats with curved lines.

Draw closer boats larger to add the sense of distance.

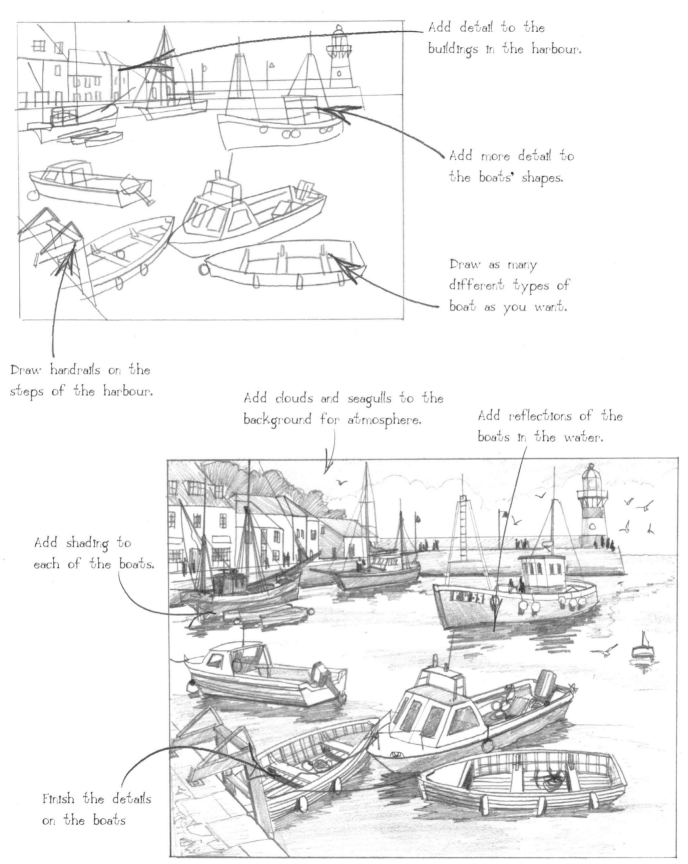

Add detail to the buildings in the harbour.

Add more detail to the boats' shapes.

Draw as many different types of boat as you want.

Draw handrails on the steps of the harbour.

Add clouds and seagulls to the background for atmosphere.

Add reflections of the boats in the water.

Add shading to each of the boats.

Finish the details on the boats

Remove any unwanted construction lines.

Glossary

Bow   The front of a boat or ship.

Composition   The positioning of a picture on the drawing paper.

Construction lines   Guidelines used in the early stages of a drawing, usually erased later.

Hold   The part of a ship where the cargo is stored.

Hull   The main body of a boat or ship.

Keel   The ridge that runs along the bottom of the hull.

Light source   The direction from which the light seems to come in a drawing.

Negative space   The empty space left between objects or parts of objects.

Perspective   A method of drawing in which the faraway parts of a scene are shown smaller than the nearer parts, to give a realistic impression of depth.

Rudder   The hinged flap at the stern of a boat that is used to steer it.

Squaring up   Enlarging a drawing using a grid of squares.

Stern   The rear of a boat or ship.

Three-dimensional   Having an effect of depth, so as to look lifelike or real.

Vanishing point   The place in a perspective drawing where parallel lines appear to meet.

Yard   A horizontal pole attached to a mast, from which a sail is hung.

Index